The First Night Out of Eden

THE FIRST NIGHT OUT OF EDEN

Jennifer Bates

University Press of Florida

*Gainesville Tallahassee Tampa Boca Raton
Pensacola Orlando Miami Jacksonville*

Copyright 1998 by the Board of Regents of the State of Florida
Printed in the United States of America on acid-free paper
All rights reserved

03 02 01 00 99 98 C 6 5 4 3 2 1

03 02 01 00 99 98 P 6 5 4 3 2 1

Library of Congress Cataloging-in-Publication Data

Bates, Jennifer (Jennifer Alice), 1968–
The first night out of Eden / Jennifer Bates.
p. cm.—(University of Central Florida contemporary poetry series)
ISBN 0-8130-1596-0 (cloth: alk. paper).—
ISBN 0-8130-1597-9 (pbk.: alk. paper)
I. Title. II. Series: Contemporary poetry series (Orlando, Fla.)
PS3553.A82723F57   1998
811'.54—dc21   97-46987

The University Press of Florida is the scholarly publishing agency
for the State University System of Florida, comprising Florida
A & M University, Florida Atlantic University, Florida Interna-
tional University, Florida State University, University of Central
Florida, University of Florida, University of North Florida,
University of South Florida, and University of West Florida.

University Press of Florida
15 Northwest 15th Street
Gainesville, FL 32611
http://nersp.nerdc.ufl.edu/~upf

*For my parents, Stanley and Virginia Bates,
who were brave enough to raise a poet,
and for my sister, Elisabeth Bates,
who has been there all along.*

*The woman answered the serpent, "We may eat the fruit of
any tree in the garden, except for the tree in the middle of
the garden; God has forbidden us either to eat or to touch
the fruit of that; if we do, we shall die." The serpent said,
"Of course you will not die. God knows that as soon as you
eat it, your eyes will be opened and you will be like gods
knowing both good and evil." When the woman saw that
the fruit of the tree was good to eat, and that it was pleasing
to the eye and tempting to contemplate, she took some and
ate it. She also gave her husband some and he ate it. Then
the eyes of both of them were opened and they discovered
that they were naked . . .*

GENESIS 3:2–7.

Contents

Acknowledgments

Some of the poems in this manuscript have appeared or are forth-
  coming in the following magazines:

The Hollins Critic: "In This New Life"
Mostly Maine: "Between Sisters," "To a Friend Whose Work Has
  Come to This"
Parting Gifts: "What I Have to Offer"
Plainsongs: "Ash Wednesday," "Getting it Back"
Report to Hell: "Good Friday," "Grandiosity," "The Survivor,"
  "A True War Story"
Twisted Nipples: "Deception," "Knowledge," "One Night Stand"

Waiting for the Hurricane

Something begs to break—
I'm riddled with nerves that measure
the air's electric body
as it presses against mine.
I pace these rooms, drawing
shades against the heat.
Outside, clouds pile, turn yellow.
The fan thrums, its rattling beat
like a heart that can't be trusted.
In South Carolina, my sister
crouches on the bathroom floor
with a flashlight, diabetic's kit,
her Bible and a loaf of bread.
Earlier, she called, her voice
wading across the wires until
the line went dead.
Outside, the wind gathers,
slamming an open door.
The blue oil ticks in my wrists.
If Hugo hits, with his bluster
and heavy blows, I'm crawling
into the closet, a candle
clutched in one chilly hand.
Also, this sheet of paper,
to hold like a shield between
myself and all that darkness,
all that water, rising and falling.

The Survivor

She has dreamed of this for years,
swaddling her fear of the dark
with a white sheet pulled across her face.
She likes to think he sees it, too,
that somewhere a man in middle age
finds himself ripped from sleep to shriek
at the doorway where she stands.
He shrieks again. He sees the woman
coming across the floor
steadily, teeth bared and shining.
Is she an animal or something human?
Her hair is a hood of flame.
Who touches her will burn.
She moves so slowly, he could run,
but he's paralyzed.
He looks into her narrowed eyes
and cannot turn.
She walks on, scarred arms outstretched
to take him in against her ribs
where she has worn
his fingerprints for years.
One hand swings up to bruise
his face, his parted lips.
This silences the scream.
Touching him lightly now,
her bloodied hand cradles and soothes.
All she wants
are the sighs escaping swiftly from him,
last sounds of a man
held by a woman
with nothing left to lose.

In the Provisional World

When the Lord closes a door, no window opens.
Decisions are made by refusing to decide.
She kicks the sheets to the foot of the bed.
Weeks later, she'll notice that no one
has pulled them smooth, just as no one
emptied the bottle on the window sill
until the wine soured to a bitter cloud.
She's on her own now. The phone is full
of wrong numbers, colors run in the wash,
and a cat shrieks all night long. In the blue
dove-pecked light at dawn, a kiss
precludes love, is not prelude.

The Plight of Daughters

That night, I woke in time
to cup my hands against my lip
and catch the loosened blood that rolled
like honey down my face. Dizzy,

I rose and tottered to the bathroom,
scattering petals of scarlet on the tiles.
The white walls pitched back
the fluorescent light, and the mirror

loomed like a giant coin, all silver
and crowded with images. Pressing
tissues against my nose, I knelt
against the doors below the sink.

Like a good machine gone wrong,
my body leaked its expensive grease.
When I pulled the tissues away,
they had swollen into a glistening heart

that seemed to pulse in my hand.
I remembered the fairy tale by Grimm
where all a young girl's protection lay
in three drops of blood on a cambric scrap

that praised her and gave her useful advice,
mourned for her when her mother could not.

Ash Wednesday

In the midst of malls, blank space.
A girl stands with her puzzled face
tilted toward the rich river of cars

while the wind tugs sharply at her hair.
She would pull off the rings she wears
and toss them onto the chilly grass;

she is willing to shed her heavy coat
like a superfluous skin, but of what use
can this possibly be if her body stays

intact? If her weak flesh refuses to peel
from her bones, freeing them to be broken
and to dance? If her spirit lies sealed

beneath a layer of dust like a dish
too fine for everyday use, locked away
behind wood and glass? If her heart remains

stubborn, intractable and red; a fist
raised against the February sky;
a smoldering rose still uncrushed to ash?

On the Road to the Cemetery

                              Mostly faithless,
nonetheless, because we have come to pay respects,
each woman has covered her head and arms.
My Turkish scarf snags on my glasses' frame.
Under my sleeves, the scars
hum their reproaches in the silence
where the family has stopped its cries
now that the coffin is leaving,
trundled across the damp earth.
Four years ago, this boy was stopped
on his way to college by an oncoming car.
Together, he and his mother
dragged a partial future out of pure refusal.
It ended yesterday.

I've been crazy in six different countries, but nothing
compares to this. At home, my cat has made a nest
in the basket on the floor of my bedroom closet.
While we step delicately over the dirt,
he beds down among my stockings and slips,
burrowing deep in the fragrant darkness.
He has never been so happy. And I never, I swear,

thought death would be like that.
I didn't dream of a slender woman, her face a flower
as she bent to fold my face in her skirt.
I didn't look for the handsome stranger,
his blue eyes gleaming in the light that bled
under my bedroom door.
When they shovel dirt onto the coffin,
I shudder like anyone living,
wanting to say, I'm sorry,
wanting to say, please, understand,

what wakes me at three a.m.
and sets me clawing at the dark
is a small girl with milky breath
and a choke collar dangling from her neck.
She brings her face in close.
She bares her teeth. She says:
Where were you? I hate this. I want to go home.

What the Trees Said

They got right down to it
in tones that shaded from green to yellow.
I shrank, I tried to keep
my innocent shoulders
clean of their shadows,
their rough-barked laughter,
but they filled the air
with their rustle and buzz.
Little sister, don't think we don't see you.
Little sister, time to be moving,
got to hustle, got to
straighten up and fly right
out of this world. Little sister,
we're waiting.

Who can resist a world gone wrong?
My roses are dying.
I haven't watered them in weeks.
I'm afraid of the back yard,
the grass dangerous under my feet.
Everything that grows is alive;
still, my roses remain what they are:
every whorled cluster of petals
cradling its lustral scent like a child
who shares in spite of herself.
They are as real as a rock in my sandal,
as a sliver of lime in a Coke.
If I could, I'd choose
these bits of lively silk,

but the trees loom. They laugh.
They grip down into the earth;
they are saying: *Little sister,*

time to be leaving.
You've been a long time coming,
and we've been waiting so long.
It would be easy to follow them now,
their voices a blur that erodes my bones,
but I'm listening for the absence of words,
the no voice when the roses say,
Little mother, come home.

Explanations: Eurydice to Orpheus

Isn't it always your story?
Your loss,
Your pain, even,
My lover, your beautiful guilt.
Did you ask if I wanted that?
Did you
Cry *Love, my only one,*

Come back, for I am lost, I am
A man
Without a path
Finding his way back home?
Listen, I've made this place my own.
At ease,
A citizen of Hell,

I know the boundaries. And I know
The line
I cannot cross.
Cerberus licks my empty hands;
He lets me pass. He knows return
Is sure:
I must come home.

Pure coincidence, your look.
I turned.
You caught me there
And took forever on yourself
My face imprinted on the air,
Floating
Back in the tepid light,

My shoulders asserting themselves,
                 A wall
           Raised against you
And your body, your living breath.
There are no miracles in Hell,
                    Only
The piercing cries. The dead,

Stripped bare, parade their broken selves.
                 Undead,
           How could you hope
To turn your eyes toward mine, toward this
Infernal pit? You never saw
                 Me, you
Were never conquered, you

Cannot hear me now. I unhook
           Your gaze,
           Return your eyes
To the living world you cannot
Leave any more than I could leave
           This place
I've claimed, my kingdom, *yes*—

Where you are not, my Orpheus,
           Where you,
           My own, are not.

A True War Story

She's drunk, and her hands shake
as she sets her glass on the bathroom sink
and rips the cardboard package apart.
When she drags the first blade across her arm,
her shaking hands grow steady.
The blood beads up so delicately,
lining the cut like a dozen
ruby-headed corsage pins
driven deep into a satin heart.

You grow peaceful and quiet.
You never expected this beauty,
the way each bead plumps to fullness
before toppling down her wrist.
The blood is thin and warm.
It has nothing to do with you.
You can't know what brought her here,
what lifts her hand and lowers it
as the cuts pile up, shoulder to wrist.
You won't be there when she wakes, alone,
to rise and follow a trail of dried
handprints flaking from the walls.
There is only this moment.
She looks in the mirror, sees blood
smudged on her forehead like ash,
drags a bleeding arm across her face,
then dips into the blood like paint
to cover her throat and chin.

Look closer. This is what you came for.
Admit that you're grateful.
What she has done is so literal,
so absolute, the facts
accomplished in steel and skin.

Later, there will be an office, questions,
medicine and regrets, so many resolutions.
You can't know this. If there's a fog
in your head, it's not her fog
as she hurried home,
tossing glances over her shoulder.
Come. Look closer.
That which floods to the surface
rested, only seconds ago, clenched
in her stubborn heart.
Now it asks to be tasted and touched.
She lifts her wrist to her lips,
and together, you watch the mirror.
You hear a hoarse voice crack, saying
My God, it's you—cracked, saying,
This is the finest moment of my life.

To a Friend Whose Work Has Come to This

It's never been easy between us, but here
in these wicker chairs,
rain falling just beyond the screens,
your words knit the air:
reconcile suspect victim incest
No memories yet.
You're planning to write your lost story
as it unknots at your touch.

A friend once told me:
if you can't assign logical meaning
to a character in your dream,
you must assume it represents an aspect of yourself.
Dear friend, I'm still writing my story
so if I give you advice, listen only
to the thorny, cardamom-sweet
throb of empathy under my words.
Listen to my hand on your arm.

You will find that nothing
is as they told you. You will find
that nothing is as you imagined,
turning back
past the locked doors
down the narrowing passage of childhood
which once seemed an open field.

The rope of memory frays,
but the story is there, whole, at the core.
Remember, as you go,
your raveled voice speaking over the rain
as we sit here, now, in the wicker chairs,

the vaulted roof over our heads.
Remember your voice
telling me this
as I listened, and the rain.

From Fire by Fire

1. THE WAITING

She stands in the doorway,
a jointed puppet counting
the books tucked onto their shelves
and the fat chairs hunched in the dark.
The blue light from the study
casts its blessing on the rug.

But at four a.m., sleep arrives.
He takes off his hat and coat.
He walks straight to her bed
and crawls beneath the rumpled sheets,
calling into the other room,
Listen, baby, enough's enough.

She will not lie down.
The typewriter hums.
Its electric breath fills the room.
Her heart skips in her chest
where the thick hand of fatigue
has scooped and left her hollow;

she rests on elbows and knees
with her forehead bowed to the floor,
and the hand shakes her like a tree,
but the night still crouches
outside her window,
a large thing, live, and waiting.

2. PANIC

In the pit of her stomach,
the panic bird hatches.

Gaunt baby,
little phoenix,

his wings creak open
wetly, they hurt him,

being new.
His hot breath dries

the roof of her mouth,
he sucks the warmth

from her narrow veins.
He stretches his neck:

the world swings askew.
Light looms,

a broken dazzle
too bright for thinking.

For eyes to see.
Against her heart,

against liver and lungs
his coarse beak knocks.

The body locks.
There is no air, no key.

3. In the Funhouse

Mirrors line the street:
store windows, plate glass doors.

She watches her body scuttle
from frame to frame like a creature

warped by the violent pressure
of water, ton upon ton.

Escaping from each view into the next
like the proverbial fish and the frying pan,

she walks faster and faster still,
holding herself like a folded fan,

like a letter she wants to send
far away, to some foreign place,

but she can't walk out the funhouse door.

4. The Act

*The hands flutter like bad angels, finally settling: one to grip
the razor, a tiny mirror, and one to receive it. The blade
moves so smooth and firm, she thinks. To cut the moon's
blank face. Red lines crowd her palms, a host of signatures.
Afterwards, she hides them any way she can, in pockets and
sleeves, under tables, but every time she lowers her guard,
one hand or the other turns itself over like the first card in a
poker game, ready to be picked up and played.*

5. The Choice

She has earned this story
and she tells it well,
lifting her scarred hands
like medals as she speaks

of a parking lot
where a car once stopped,
pulled off the highway
for food and gas.
There were others,
as real and solid
as a stand of trees,
but here, in the telling,
she brushes them offstage.
What matters is that girl
who stayed outside, alone,
watching the line of cars
stretch like a soiled ribbon.
Death didn't need to bargain.
He cocked his left eyebrow
and gestured with one hand
towards her landscape
as it was, the sickly
grass, the asphalt, the un-
bearable grey weather.
She was ready to stop,
to lay it down for good,
but the brute
spark in her brain
commanded her legs to move.
She circled the lot
like an obedient horse.
She waited for her name.
Someone called,
and she set one foot
in front of the other,
she moved towards him
like a girl walking,
an ordinary girl,
walking
straight into the wind.

What I Have to Offer

FOR GLENYE CAIN

So you are back from Ireland.
Your letter says you are awake,
in love, and ready for your newest life.
As always, you send invitation to visit
your small estate, drink whiskey, talk,
and let your beagle's well-shaped head
rest against my thigh. His eyes are clear.
The two of you see everything together,
except for Ireland. That sky saw you alone,
asking questions of the one you love.
The clouded darkness heard him answer
your persistence with a kissed confession.
You left, but you'll return.
Your letter asks me to nudge you now
"like a passenger on a train,"
asks me to keep you awake.

My long hair is gone, sheared off
clean across the back. I still listen
for the steely whisper behind my ears,
deep warning. I've taken to wearing rings: onyx and pearl,
a silver rhinoceros, and an opal
soft and blind as the eye of a fish
who has lived for years in the coldest depths,
shaped by fabulous pressures. Glenye,
I've been sleeping here for months,
always alone, the air so soft
on my naked neck and the absent drift of hair
no man will ever wind over his wrist again.
Not in this lifetime, anyway;

I make no promises for the next.
Your letters stay by my bed.
At night, when I take off my rings,
they rest against your words:
pearl and onyx, the silver rhinoceros,
the tiny, glinting eye.

Addictions

At first, coffee seemed less than crucial.
Then they told me my medicine meant no drinking.
I froze. No whiskey, pale fire
that drowns and keeps on burning?
No wine flooding over the bottle's lip
as rough as the Red Sea?
I hid the bottles under the sink
and considered what remained.
It's true, I'm in love
with the struck match and sulfurous whiff.
I'll let sucked smoke unfurl
from between my lips like a kept promise,
but let me open my throat for the deeper breath
and I choke, which means I cheat,
pretending it's need that wafts my hand
with its smoldering token, pretending
it's not merely gesture, this tracing
of circles in the air, this licking my lips
between drags. I can take it
or leave it, and that's the truth.
As for the obvious—call it men, or sex,
the wild sweet rumpus of the body—
that's an expense I can ill afford. Which leaves
early mornings, the kettle placed on the burner
until the steam rackets against its tin roof.
When I hoist and pour, making freshly brewed coffee,
I feel like a little Christ here in my kitchen.
Listen, they've taken the rest away,
or I've given it up, but I have this
and it's strong enough to stave off death.
Not forever. And yet—the scent of Kona
drifts over the table. Caffeine rinses my heart
with its foolish glitter, and I believe

that if some angel descends to take me
I can purchase twenty minutes at least
by saying, "O.K. But first, sit down.
Rest your wings. Let's have a cup, and then
I'll be ready to go. If you're done, that is,
and don't want more."

My Mother's Southern Accent

Not to be passed down from mother to daughter.
She dropped it in college like a boy from home,
to be played, years later, for laughs. When she slurred
her words with wet sugar and swallowed her vowels
like strawberries in champagne, all other voices
took on the stink of salt and rust.
She charmed everyone but the occasional man
who edged away when she tilted her head
and smiled, as if to say: *Of course, it's all theater.*
Just remember that I can.

As for me—what Northern child
can soften like that, even after swallowing
actual champagne. I eat strawberries standing
over the sink, and wash them down with ice water.
Still, whatever it was you meant to call me,
be careful. I have other ways of sweetening.
I am her daughter.

Good Friday

She called you Judas. You snarled denial.
Undaunted, she pressed on. I wish
I'd been the one to say it, but you can't
have everything, or so my mother told me,
and isn't the fact that someone
spit it out all that really matters?
By now, you've probably guessed:
I'm finally picking up the pieces
of the heart I claimed you never broke.
What hurt most? You lied. I believed you
for the sake of touch. And our last night,
something apart from your faithlessness—
not a crime of the heart, but a crime,
taking us beyond the country songs
I love to belt on Sundays.

Judas. Don't be so quick to dismiss.
You want forgiveness? Pay attention.
They loved each other. More than once,
Jesus brushed wayward hair from the eyes
into which he loved to look, and not
just for his own reflection. They bent
his arms as arms should not be bent. Sweat
beaded on his skin. The nails bit in,
and then the spear. Still, the cry—*Eli,
Eli, lema sabacthani*—was something else,
astonishment that so much pain
could stem from a single kiss.

Knowledge

Listen, I never wanted it.
Put me in the garden and tell me
Do not eat of the fruit of this tree
and you can bet
I'd still be combing the dirt with a stick,
unabashedly naked.
Wide-eyed, I rest in your arms, believing.
At first, this innocence is charming.
Later, you feel it insults you.
After all, it was the wall that drew you,
that vast emptiness which wound around me like a moat.
Now you've crossed, and I'm too giddy.
I've set down suspicion too easily.
Tell me lies and I lap them up.
Let me catch you
with your hand in my purse
and I'll only ask if it's enough.
Who could blame you?
When you hit me, I cower at the bed's far edge,
and what comes next will be up to you.
You can weep your pretty salt tears.
You can use words your mother has never heard
issuing from your pretty lips.
You can crook your finger slowly,
and yes, you can bring me
sidling back across the sheets
to crawl into your arms.
You can sleep heavily until dawn
while I lie, back pressed to your chest,
my teeth sinking into my wrist,
naked, ashamed, and wise.

Labyrinth

In my dream, the voices whispered,
Enter the labyrinth through the black mirror.
The coffee brims. Wreathed darkness. Steam.
You curve your fingers to the cup and wince.
A man once touched your face like that
as he placed the word between your lips.
When Orphée snapped on rubber gloves,
the mirror yielded to his touch,
all its hard silver splintered to water.
He pushed through, going down for love,
Eurydice, his wife, and Death.
He loved Death's face, the way its steel
shuddered and softened when she looked at him.
Eurydice was dearest to him in death:
the prize he'd sing for, do anything.
Offscreen, she was colder than Cocteau knew,
coldly selfish and bored with this walk.
The men we've known also got it wrong.
Tell me, he asked you by the cemetery wall,
where you sat on the sunny morning after,
Tell me, was that rape?
I've told you, how I pressed against his shoulder,
tried to slow my breath, and watched him sleep.
He tells it differently: *That night, you came to my room,*
kissed me, and I watched you sleep.
I've seen your nightmares, another said.
I've seen what happens in your sleep.
When I trace the mirrored outline of my face,
the bright glass makes my fingers stumble.
In your dream, Eurydice gave the look.
Orpheus went out like a candle.

The First Night Out of Eden

I.

All the books will say I did it. But you betrayed me too! I
hungered with a buzz in the head, an empty place demanding
to be filled, and I know your skull rang with the same call.
Nights you whispered again and again, in the tender dark, *O
my hunger.* The new mosquito whined in my ear, then bit. A
sting. A kiss. He opened me. You slapped him down, the tiny
smear of blood on my throat you licked clean. Later, the
perfect fruit in my open hand, your eyes dropped and you bent
over my palm, tongue to the rosy skin. I looked into your
innocent eyes, felt the itch at my throat and let you graze in
the poisonous orchard I had become. Laying my free hand
against your face, I lifted your dripping chin. I loved you. I love
you still but I cannot bear to look at you crumpled, a small
leaf under His feet. Does His face turn from mine? A large
light, tell me, does it shine upon me still? See, I bend at the
knees, drop to the ground, set my forehead against damp earth.
Love, I have come down after you. Stand and raise me up.

2.

Pebbles crunch beneath our feet
and your arm on my shoulders
anchors me to the path
as my hand touches your side,
cupping the place where the first scar formed.
We stumble beneath the moon,
who does not smile.
A large eye, she looks hard,
the one clear thing shining
in a sky choked with clouds.

Where are we?
Is there a wind?
Already you have converted
to a life of difficult tasks.
You prepare yourself
for labors, for sweat and pain.
I gasp, try to suck the last
innocence from the air.
Are there words for this?
You who named the animals,
you who named me, speak,

for now my tongue and lips
have locked all speech away.
Once I thought you were hewn from light,
a brightness always before me.
Even now you draw me
back towards the center.
You stand between myself
and the long door now opening
out of the night to receive me.
Like a gaping mouth, it waits,
one more wound in the side of the dark.

Halo

Last spring, you dreamed yourself a saint,
another Catherine broken on the wheel.
Living on water and delusion,
you nourished yourself with portraits
of martyrs in the local museum.
You ran without purpose or ceasing
like some rat in an experimenter's maze
until the depression gripped you,
forcing you down on your knees.

Locked in your frantic cycle,
you tried to escape your body for good.
You fed yourself the bitter food
of fifty sedatives and went to sleep.
Waking to doctors in a white room,
you couldn't believe you had risen
to the light of one more day.
To you, that room is a second prison
you must somehow try to escape.

Where you are now was once all farms.
Instead of the bony hospital, perhaps
a huge barn rested its dusty frame.
Bathed in a cloud of chaff and dim light,
the oxen trod their inevitable path
around and around the open floor.
Their iron feet beat a circle in place,
and their haunches moved like giant wheels,
groaning beneath their bodies' weight.

The oxen have all disappeared.
And still, in your sleep, you hear
the thudding. Does it comfort you,

who can only travel the circle
you pace in your small white room?
You are pacing it now, my broken saint,
with the air around your head
beaten tighter than gold, and your face
turned in shadow like the moon.

Grandiosity

I didn't ask to be Christ. It just happened.
The cloud of fire roosted in my head
and there I was, a blunt dazzle.
This just after I had finally located
the border of the intolerable,
the day I walked out into the sun
and pain came thick upon me
like a swarm of razor blades with wings.
I checked my ankles and wrists:
no holes, but I found
a tangle of stretchmarks on each hip
and pale lines crossing my breasts—
scars previously without purpose—
and hadn't I already died

at the hands of someone who loved me?
Something opened inside my head
and my cruel flock took to the sky.
Every cup, every crumb meant communion.
The door hummed as I approached;
it could open onto anything.
When I took its brass knob in my hand,
the drawing forth and the shutting behind
were fraught with meaning and mysterious.
Now I am learning again to be human.
Coffee is still a small sacrament,
but the door opens and closes in silence,
it means what it is.

Persephone Below, or What Keeps Her There

1.

The aching thighs
Death's handmaids wash
with rags dipped in Lethe.
The bruises and the healed flesh
please him equally.

2.

The flowers he knocked from her breasts
that first day, above ground,
pressed in her diary.

3.

The seven seeds of the pomegranate, crushed between her teeth.

4.

His enormous cock and balls, dangling in front of her face.
He asks, does size matter?
I don't know, she says.

5.

She knows her mother is searching, will find her.
Not sooner or later. When.

6.

Above, on earth again, she dances with the young men,
                              cleaving the air like a sword.
One walks her home at dawn.
They pause in the road.

7.

Death waits for her with roses,
pale and beaded with dew.
She takes him in her mouth
before he has asked her to.
In the morning, she waves the handmaids away.
She asks for fruit.

Said the Patient to the Psychiatrist

You want to hear
about the severed hand I saw on the street,
wrist neatly trimmed and long bled dry,
and how it shifted back
to last night's smashed pumpkin
when I forced myself to look again.
Or the way the trees dipped toward me,
a story about me moving
from leaf to leaf
like the synaptic leap between nerves.

Who sees what when you see the sea?
Sometimes my mouth fills with blood.
I walk with that oily bloom
gagging me, mouth open and saliva strung
across my lapel in sticky pearls.

No. No. You think all this is metaphor?
I am the water and the weir.
God baits his hook with me.
At the end of the day, he gathers my remnants.
I saw the sea, but it didn't see me.
It never ends, this music.

The Teresa Poems

*Teresa of Avila was a sixteenth-century mystic, born in 1515.
At the age of sixteen, she was sent to board at a convent after
a potentially scandalous love affair. She entered the Carmelite
order in 1553. During her first years, she suffered a debilitating
illness. At one point, she was declared dead: a grave was pre-
pared and her eyes sealed with wax. She was to survive, al-
though for the next twenty years she felt herself increasingly
torn between the call of the world and the call of God.*

1. Entering the New Year

The year the blood showed up,
the year my mother died,
I turned my back on Christ
and all my pieties.
I learned to wash myself
like a bowl of fruit, polishing
my limbs with a soapy cloth.
I softened my hands with lotion.
I shook out my hair like a shawl,
admired its glossy threads
and pinned it high, exposing
the curves of chin and brow.

And the perfumes in little bottles!
They were better than a tonic.
I anointed myself at throat and wrists
and my temple, where the blood leaps
in the vein like a little fish.
I wanted to lie down
in a field full of grass, near a pond
languid with lilies.
All day, I lapped up the scent.

The slap of sandals against the ground . . .
picture me as I sway
through Avila's dusty streets,
tossing words to the boys trailing me.
Notice the tilt of my thirsty hips,
my eyes like a pair of wells,
my face as white as paper
and my dress the color of flame—
as if I had torn the heated skin
off the sun to clothe myself.
Watch me walk beneath that naked eye
burning, burning, burning.

2. Teresa Succumbs

And so I fell. Sixteen, and ripe
as a dozen apples, I tumbled
into Satan's steaming mouth,
panting and nestling there.

Then the talk began—a hundred
tongues clapping and waving.
I had gone out dressed in honor,
my honor, all that I had.
The gossips turned aside,
baring their teeth as I passed.
I was in the hand of danger.
He smiled and shut my eyes,
sealing them with a kiss.

He was not for sale.
My father tried and tried,
searching for a husband,
a way to save my pride.
Dear man, how he loved me.
Dear God, how I lied.

3. CONVENT

They shut me up with nuns
to save my damaged name.
Cells and stone walls framed
my new accomplishments:
reading, writing, the Catechism,
lace-making and mandolins . . .

Husband or habit. Choose.
I tried. I tried. Took daily
the Host between my teeth.
Satan fumbling for my heart
with fingers ringed in ice
would have found only stone
cracked slightly to reveal
the salty rind beneath.

Nightly, I watched a curtain
of red silk rise in the air
above the foot of my bed.
A thick snout stirred
the rich folds, lifting
the fringed hem to offer
its heavy head for the stroking,
the boldest touch. For the love.

The hot breath warmed my cheek.
Husband or habit. I chose.
Father said no.
I left his house at dawn,
my bones wrenched in their sockets
and shaken loose.
Finding the convent door, I bruised
my knuckles with my knock.

4. THE SENTENCE

i.

a dozen knives
wedged in my back

a shower of blows
from crown to soles

fever heating the brain
each succulent limb

withering like grass

ii.

they scour the body
draw off tainted blood

bitter herbs
the daily purge

water rusts on my tongue
thrust back, a warm flood

all bread is ash

iii.

I lie down in filth
and do not rise

the thing in my chest
shakes itself, sharpens

its claws on my ribs
gnaws at the salty stone

drooling, and licks its lips

iv.

O God, unhook
Achilles' cord

draw out bone
peel back the skin

crack hinges wide, undo
my heels, my knees

I burn I burn

v.

an electric sea
my mouth fills

the unrooted tongue
batters against the teeth

the fragile walls
I swallow lovingly

(the seizure's host)

vi.

to wake in a dark place
eyes sealed

already a grave waits
I lift my hands

peel the wax from my face
in wafers   like cracked coins

counterfeits
                    little ghosts

5. Little Lazarus

This rude awakening
hurt me like a sword.
So sensitive, I winced
against the simple light—
they lifted me by grasping
the four corners of a sheet.

St. Joseph healed me.
Not like Peter, the shadow
stretching over filthy beds
to brush each believer,
sucking away sickness
in one swift breath.

Even shadows weigh too much . . .
curled, knees to chest,
I shiver beneath the wind.
A small singing, it blows,
lightly away, the dust.
One finger moves.

But nothing lasts forever.
Spring comes. I cross
the floor on hands and knees,
thanking God. Months pass,
and I unfold my limbs,
a wooden doll tossed

back into the clatter
(Doña Teresa de Ahumada
is wanted in the parlor)
of gossip, perfumes, pets,
and the company of men.

I know nothing but how to talk.

6. Ecce Homo

Twenty years. My father's death.
He died like an angel.

My sisters primp before confession.
Absolution is bought as cheaply as a kiss.

I have dreamed myself as Magdalene,
washing His feet in my tears—

Dona Teresa de Ahumada is wanted in the parlor.

The *Ecce Homo,* a gaudy gift
someone left out in the hall:

Christ covered with wounds.
The pallid flesh, the crown of thorns,

and blood wetting His cheeks
and blood flowing from His side

and blood congealed and blackening
along the lines of the whip . . .

Dear my Lord, what have they done?

Dear my Lord, you are broken indeed

and breaking behind my ribs
something

        shatters

something

       shudders

        steadies

       slows

I touch my face

                press

salty fingers

                against my breast

and turn, half falling

                into the air

blowing through this stone corridor,

                into the outstretched arms.

To the North Pole: Louise Boyd

As a child in Marin County,
I fought the heat by placing
slivers of ice on my tongue.
Now I have entered the kingdom
of winter and hidden water.
Massive fields of solid ice—
as if invisible hands
had spread ream upon ream
of paper, beautifully blank.

North, north, north we flew
into the eye of the needle
contorted beneath the compass's glass.
Like Jacob wrestling with the angel,
it writhes, it will not cease,
aiming for the source.

Life Sentence

1.

Neurology was empty except for me
and the man sitting three chairs away.
Standing, he would have come to my waist.
We spoke lightly, carefully.
When he said, "I used to be six feet tall,"
I nodded in confused sympathy.
He flushed and said, "I'm joking."

2.

Inside I was asked to squat on my heels
and stand suddenly, to close my eyes and bring
one finger to the tip of my nose. Was my cycle
"normal"? How frequently did my olfactory
hallucinations—those sudden mouthfuls
of vomit or blood—occur?
It wasn't far from there
to prescriptions and humorous banter.

I thought: this man should be selling cars.
He had a smile that spread like sunset
over the roof of Somerville Auto Parts:
"After all, if you get too manic,
you could end up very poor.
You get too depressed—" and here
the smile disappeared, and he raised
his hands palms up as if to offer
the final rebate, the clinching incentive—

3.

On Tegretol, I shuffled, listing to the left
and slurring my words. I stopped
taking the pills the day I started

walking into walls. I can't tell you
what I learned, leaning there.
The brick was rougher than a stubbled cheek.
The only thought left to think
was "I don't have to take this,"
and after that I didn't.

4.

What happened next bores me to repeat.
Suffice to say, now I take what I have to,
so that I can come home
and kneel with my wool coat spreading around me
like Ophelia's waterlogged gown.
As I meet the cat nose to nose,
I can close my fingers around
the black furled bud of his paw.
I can hold the five flexed thorns.

All Hallows' Eve

We three jostle
like eggs in a paper bag,
elbowing each other,
barking jokes.
Two men and a woman
who are not in love
can notice together
how the black sky glistens,
how rain has licked the street,
how a trick of light
unlocks the clouds
and bloodies the innocent moon.

Deception

The first time, I was stupid.
Nursed a single rose
and two letters across the Atlantic,
left them shredded
in a hotel wastebasket.
The next man who comes my way
won't have it so easy.
When I reach for his wrists,
the nerves jumping in my fingertips
are the wires of a polygraph.
When I kiss,
my tongue probes,
searching for lies
trapped between his teeth
like scraps of meat
after the banquet.
He leaves the bedroom
and pads down the hall to pee,
and I've got my hand
deep in the drawer of the bedside table.
He'll return to find me
sprawled under the rumpled sheets—
naked, what could I be hiding?
I'm dazed and drowsy,
and the room has its usual disorders,
no traces of disruption—
oh, I'll be warm and open,
as natural as cookies and milk
while I'm hitching a stocking to my garter belt,
adjusting the strap on my slip.
I'll sit on the edge of his bed fully dressed,
sweep my hand over his back,
drop a kiss. Maybe two.

Then it's back to the living room.
I put on my wrinkled trenchcoat,
pat the pockets for cigarettes
and make my way out to the street.
Briefly, the flare of a match studs the dark.
I lean against a street lamp
and smoke. Wisps of mist
streak the sky's fathomless blue.
I'll have one ear cocked
for the creak of a door,
an unfamiliar foot on the sill;
my eyes will rest on the gloomy panes
as I wait for the flicked switch.
For hurried footsteps.
The true rendezvous.

In This New Life

I have colored my lips
and brushed new shadows
in the hollows over my eyes.
Anything to distract
from the gap in my side
where someone once laid his hand.
Now there's nothing there,
only the old wound mending.
I have bent to brush my hair,
letting it sweep the floor.
Tonight I stood, shook out
the sparks. No one was there.

Looking for Your Life

FOR W.

More than hunger, it's thirst that drives you.
You have nothing to slake that parched throat,
no rain slashing against your window,
no dew slicked on the fat pears
that grow out back in the garden,
miraculous in this barren city.
You can't pinpoint the moment
when Disaster came to stand beside you,
dipped her great head and licked your neck.
Tears might help, but you have no tears.
When you wake, cast up from terror
as from the silty ocean,
the sweat that coats your body
dries to a bitter residue.
So you touch the blade to your soft arm,
draw forth a different water.
I understand, but it isn't an answer,
just salt and rust on the tongue.

One Night Stand

A brisk tenderness costs you nothing.
Take this body, sick with holiness,
ease my saintly patience.
Turn me over and over
like a word you'll keep on your lips forever.
Make me a room I am always leaving . . . .
I don't ask you to look down and find
something you can't do without,
or draw your hand to old bruises.
When I refuse to give my name,
you get to call me anything.
Hush. Let me kneel
and fit two bodies together
with an acolyte's precision.
Outside your window
a bat nips and flaps at the darkness.
The moon has been dirtied with milk.
It's an odd hour. That's all.
If I leave here with something more—
crumpled bills slipped from your wallet,
or the watch you unstrapped and laid
carelessly on the bedside table—
it only frees us further.
An altar is an altar is an altar.
Please. It's not personal.

Almost an Elegy

Nothing should have come from nothing.
I was not your mother.
I would not have been.
If I turn now, if I stretch my hand
back into that darkness,
I am only a tourist at the site of disaster.
Orpheus descended, not for love,
but because he refused to go on living
without knowing the story's end.

Those nights that made you,
strangers emptied themselves
of all but the shapes of their gestures:
a boy stretched out on a narrow bed,
the girl kneeling beside him
to cast her body like a fisherman's net,
radiant with delusion.
He who loses his life, etc.
Fishers of men.

Later, desperate to shed you,
my heated body knelt again,
not prophet, not saint,
just God's kicked dog,
dragging myself belly down to wait
against the tiled wall until our brief
introduction was complete.
You undid yourself back to the beginning
and left me your absence

in which to lower my skirt and stand,
both hands gripping the sink.
I can't say who you would have been.
Had you lived, you would stand to inherit

the cat, pearls, a double bed,
ten thousand in life insurance
and (perhaps) the crossed wires in my head
which keep me running like a faulty clock,
like Orpheus ascending, foolish singer

who failed to remember the future—
how long it is, how unforgiving—
towards which he climbed as if in a dream,
trembling, smiling, thinking *It's over.
Nothing left but the song.*

Makeup

In her black slip and stockings, my mother
speaks over her shoulder, saying
The trick with makeup is to look
as if you're not wearing any. She fastens
diamonds in her ears and dabs perfume
on the pulses of her throat and wrists.

At ten, I know this is not the whole story.
Leaning into the mirror, she hollows
her cheeks, dusting shadows across her face
and under the jaw, showing me
how to cheat the eye into believing
that the angles of age have been softened
and the lines of the face drawn true.
When she's finished, she holds the little brush
like a thin cigarette; she taps it against
her makeup case, and a cloud of blush
rises like smoke in the fragrant air.

I sit on the edge of the bed, watching her
as she uncaps a stick of kohl.
She draws lines of grey that she smudges
with the tip of her little finger.
She smooths silver across her eyelids
and fans ivory in wide delicate wings
to trap light beneath her brows.
It's a question of shapes and shadows:
the arrangement of light and dark.

This is not the whole story.
When she raises her lipstick to her mouth,
I need to know where the color falls
in the litany of names—Lavender Ice,
Cherries in the Snow, Silk Champagne—

and I want those words closer than breath
against my lips. Each name is locked
in its waxy base, a seal she sets
on her face, to leave on every cup
she'll drink from, every face she'll kiss.

In the Garden

1.

And the Lord God caused a deep sleep
to fall upon Adam, and he slept:
and He took one of his ribs . . . .
But what did He do then?
Did He start with clean cartilage,
or was the Lord forced
to scrub His bony prize?
Did He breathe once to bring her forth,
or was it hours He spent
pinching the folds in her brain,
knitting the pouch of her lungs,
kneading her fat heart?

2.

She shall be called Woman, because
she was taken out of Man . . . .
Nameless, she roamed the garden,
following Adam from tree to tree.
She opened her mouth obediently
to swallow the food he offered:
berries and broad green leaves.
He assigned her little jobs:
weeding, picking flowers.
She knelt where he pointed.
She drank from the Euphrates
and did not converse with God.

3.

Eat, said the serpent,
whipping his tail like a cane.
He looked straight into her eyes.
Ye shall not surely die.

Your eyes shall be opened,
and ye shall be as gods . . . .
An odor she did not recognize
drifted from his scales,
a blend of sulphur and rain.
Eat, daughter, he said.
Your God is a jealous God.
Eat, and learn your name.

4.

Because it was spring forever there.
Because words dropped from the serpent's mouth
and lay in the soft dirt, shining.
She gathered them in her hands
where they clinked together.
She never expected the silver
spilling from Adam's lips:
The woman whom thou gavest to be with me,
she gave me of the tree, and I did eat . . . .
She didn't know they would have to leave.
She wanted to feed him well.
And Adam called his wife's name Eve.

5.

And I will put enmity between thee and the woman . . . .
The serpent smirked. Adam shut his eyes.
Already the hunger pangs
clamored in Eve, a cramping ache.
God raised her chin. She blinked.
Daughter, He said, you have eaten
pain, and pain is your lodger now,
to nourish and to know.
You must pick up this emptiness.
You must carry it away.
He withdrew His hands,
turned His face, and let her go.

At the Animal Hospital

A weimaraner trots through the waiting room,
a wound almost six inches long
stitched across his throat.
He's wearing a plastic funnel
wrapped around his head like a lampshade,
but he's happy and going home.
Another man murmurs to the whiskered face
poking out sideways from under his coat,
mewing softly underneath the sign:
"ALL ANIMALS MUST BE RESTRAINED
IN A CARRIER OR ON A LEASH."
I've got an empty carrier,
as does the woman at the front desk.
She's discussing cremation with the cashier.
She wants to pick up the ashes;
she doesn't want them mailed.
Her high heels click on the linoleum
as she shifts to dig for a tissue in her purse,
and we lucky ones look away.
In a pamphlet, I read that cats outnumber dogs
by five million in the United States.
My cat is somewhere inside,
his black fur ruffled and damp,
his small sides heaving with recovered breath
behind doors I'm not allowed through.
The taxi is waiting.
Outside in the falling snow,
the streetlamps' light blurs to blue
and each minute strikes the sidewalk like a match,
then sputters to smoldering damp.
I pet the basset hound under my feet
and chat with the woman beside me.

We've almost forgotten why we came
when the attendant brings out the wire cage
and my seatmate turns to me and exclaims,
There he is. There's your baby.

Yes to Hats, No to Shoulder Bags

. . . is to come home to an empty room,
pull the shades and peel off my dress,
letting it drift to the floor as I step
free of my high-heeled shoes
and slide into the mirror's embrace.
I'm down to perfume, my stockings and my slip,
white flesh, black lace—clichés
are clichés because they're true.
Someone said that. Someone
also said that my eyes are palest
blue and streaked with lightning.
Curious? Guess. I'm not telling.
And I won't shower or change. Not to eat,
not to play solitaire. I'll just lie on the couch
like a cat, like the dead, like a long-stemmed rose,
with dirty dishes piled at my feet. Anything
could happen while I'm smelling my wrists.
Anything. Anything.

Between Sisters

Pulled from my box
with the bills (white

paper, slick windows),
your thick blue square.

My name in your script.
Where I live written

in your bold hand,
your name lodged above mine.

Blue folded within blue.
Chinese boxes? Russian dolls?

Black upon blue.
Tiny letters, tiny tracks

in a field of blue snow.
Your hand on the page.

Your hand in Scotland
writing, folding—

the stamp touches your tongue.
You lick your lips,

satisfied, little cat—
my animal, my only one—

satisfied, like this, like that.

Revelation

All nerves and tails,
the chameleons climb
the cage's walls, turn sullen,
change direction, crawl
beneath the heated rock.
As pets, they've failed:
you cannot love them.
Still, you greet them daily,
stroking the tiny skulls,
each slender spine.

The night I came to your door
trembling, the nameless fear
trapped like a bone in my throat,
you offered what you had—
a drink, a place to sleep,
some temporary comfort.
You let me shake myself to stillness
then handed me your coat
to fold beneath my head.
Yawning, you touched my hair
and went to bed.

The heat rock hummed in the glass house.
I watched the chameleons run
back and forth, up and down,
until the smaller one
caught me, widened its gaze
and twitched its wiry tail.
As green as the electric flush
of leaves in early spring,
his pinched and wrinkled chest
pumped in and out,

an old suitcase collapsing
onto its steel frame.

How long he held me there,
I couldn't say. I made
my way to the kitchen,
seized a carving knife
and carried it back to the couch.
Gripping the dull blade
in my hand until it ached,
I lay a long time, waiting
for the dark outside the window
to go weak with early light.

The clock struck four.
Claws scrabbled near my head.
The small eyes narrowed,
pinpricks of blackness, pure
as wet paint. Closing my eyes,
I still saw that pointed face.
I touched the knife to reassure
myself. Then laid it by.

When I turned out the light,
a bright patch lingered
in the darkness near the cage.
It clung to the air,
trembling against the night.
And was, and was not there.

The Deaf Horses

I've been dreaming about the deaf horses again,
making my way to the outskirts
of the town I survived as a child.
The gravel shoulder
creaks and whimpers under my feet
as I walk along the road
past the broken stone wall,
past the covered bridge,
past the dam weeping thick sluices of water
down its face of silk cement.

I want the farm whose fields
hold the mothers and foals.
It's been seventeen years
since I gripped a barreled body with my knees;
I haven't come for that embrace.
The babies play in the grass
while the mares brush their chins
along the flexed pearls of the slender spines.

I want to touch,
standing at the barbed wire fence,
cupped hand outstretched like a supplicant at the rail.
The deaf horses nearly shatter
the dream's frame with their clarity.
They don't answer.
I'm left in my body which will never have a child.
The sun pours down, drenches us,
and we are glazed and polished to a helpless beauty
until I'd recognize the deaf horses anywhere.
Waking. A little later on, asleep.

Jennifer Bates, who lives in Massachusetts, recently completed her first novel and will receive her MFA from Emerson College in 1998.